THE CHILDREN'S SERMON

CHRISTIAN CLASSICS *for* YOUNG READERS

THE CHILDREN'S SERMON

with a Selection of
Five Minute Sermons
to Children,
for Pastors, Sunday-School Libraries
and Home Reading

by

The REV. JOHN C. HILL

With an introduction for preachers by
Timothy Matthew Slemmons

This edition, including Introduction, Book Design, and Cover Photo
© 2018 Christian Classics for Young Readers. All rights reserved.

First reprint edition

PRINTED IN THE UNITED STATES OF AMERICA
9 8 7 6 5 4 3 2 1

ISBN-13: 978-1546466406
ISBN-10: 1546466401

"Ye shall teach them your children!" —
Deuteronomy 11:19

Contents

An Introduction for Preachers　　　xi

PREFACE　　　xxi

Part I
THE SERMON

1

I. Who Started It?	3
II. What Is It?	4
III. *Cui bono?*	5
IV. How Is It Done?	8
V. How Begin?	9
VI. When?	10
VII. Every Sabbath?	11

Part II
THE SERMONS

13

1. Daisies And Buttercups	15
2. Burdock And Thistles	19
3. Snow	23
4. Sin .	28
5. Sin Forgiven	31
6. Prayer	36
7. Walking With God	41
8. The Lamp	45
9. A Boy Who Walked With God	49
10. Not Your Own	53
11. Who Is On The Lord's Side?	57
12. Christ's Invitation To His Supper	61
13. The Lord's Supper	66
14. Working for Jesus	70
15. Going to Church	74
16. The Bible	78

An Introduction for Preachers

This sweet, unpretentious little book, by the Rev. John C. Hill, is one I have had on my shelf for several years. I expect there are still a few dusty copies dozing undisturbed in any number of church libraries. Originally published in 1882, in Philadelphia, by the Trustees of the Presbyterian Board of Publication, it bore the full title, *The Children's Sermon, with a Selection of Five Minute Sermons to Children, for Pastors, Sunday-School Libraries and Home Reading*, and the biblical epigraph: *"Ye shall teach them your children!"*, absent the citation of Deuteronomy 11:19 that appears above.

Now, a hundred thirty-six years after its initial publication, it seems fitting to make it available once again for several reasons.

First, this book stands, with but a few other titles mentioned by the author, at or very near the headwaters of the children's sermon "movement," which he refers to as such in the opening sentence of Part I. What he intends, however, is not so much a general recommendation of all the books of sermons to children from which the 19th c. suffered no lack, sermons that were common features of Sunday evening services and other youth-oriented assemblies. Rather, he notes in particular the shortening of the children's sermon so as to include it as an additional element, along with the customary sermon in the main Sunday worship service. Thus, while he mentions J. G. (James Griswold) Merrill's *Twenty-Five Sermons to the Children of the Congregational Church of Davenport, IA* (1878), he does not mention the much earlier and longer *Sermons for Children*, by another Merrill, Maine preacher Josiah G. Merrill, "pastor of a church in Cape Elizabeth." That volume, from 1837, would seem to stand apart from and well ahead of the movement Hill has in mind, as would J. C. Ryle's

Sermons for Children (1856), and *Two Bears, and Other Sermons for Children* (1869), each of which sermons stretch to some twenty pages.

In the post-war decades, other collections emerged from the likes of Richard Newton, John Ellison, J. M. Neale, Mark Guy Pierce, James Vaughan, William Wilberforce Newton (the son of Richard), Wilbur F. Crafts, one J. Gregg, and others, including what appears to be the sole "method," by Henry Clay Trumbull, *Children in the Temple* (1869). With the aim of distinguishing the short form, Hill especially recommends reading and imitating the style or "spirit" of (Richard) Newton, Pastor of St. Paul's Episcopal Church, Philadelphia, whom no less than Charles Spurgeon dubbed "the Prince of Preachers to children," and whose son (William Wilberforce Newton) was nearly as prolific as his father. Concurrent with the delivery of Hill's own sermons, John Norton issued a volume in 1881.

It is only just and fitting, however, to acknowledge earlier pioneers of the genre whom Hill does not mention: Philip Doddridge who, in the 18th c., seems to have been the first to make the children's sermon a priority; while Rebecca Wilkinson,—as early as 1789!—anonymously published her collection *Sermons to Children; to Which are Added Short Hymns, Suited to the Subjects*, bearing the scant attribution, "By a lady." Early though they were, Wilkinson's sermons, like Hill's, belong to the short form, and moreover were popular enough to fuel demand for no less than seven editions in the ensuing decades.

The early decades of the 19th c. saw, in addition to reprints of Wilkinson, volumes by Alexander Fletcher, John Burder, Zechariah Taft, Samuel Nott, Cornelius Roosevelt Duffie, and Merrill (of Maine), all of which testify, in one way or another, to the church's attempt to honor the priority that Jesus placed on children in the kingdom.

This is not the place to analyze or critique these works, but simply to note the rising wave—including at least one in feminine dress, nearly a century earlier—of what Hill would come to discern and describe as a movement toward including the children in the main Sunday service with a sermon of their own. Meanwhile, in 1882, the author reckoned less than 200 churches across the country were offering such children's sermons, and his stated aim here is clearly to encourage others to do the same.

For the sake of historical value and interest, I have refrained from modernizing the text. Other than a handful of other very minor updates, the King James idiom has been retained, as has the preponderance of masculine language, which on more than one occasion will cause even the most traditional 21st c. reader to appreciate at least the basic aims of more inclusive language. Likewise, when he speaks of Paul's handling of the metaphor of slavery, Hill's observation that we do not have slavery in this country anymore, is startlingly brief, matter-of-fact, and incomplete, but today's reader, expecting a more thorough explanation would do well to recall that the immensely costly Civil War will have shaped the living memory of every adult in the church, to say nothing of the scars and stumps borne by those in attendance. With such enormous topics, no single sermon, least of all the children's sermon in its short form, can be expected to deal exhaustively.

By encountering the text as it is, however, the reader no doubt will be struck, not only by matters of contextual distance (e.g., we speak of "burrs" rather than "burdock"; our sidewalks no longer consist of wobbly planks, etc.), but by common elements of and insights into the children's sermon that people often observe today (e.g., the frequency with which children's sermons are more memorable than the sermon proper; the concern with short attention spans, which are apparently not as new to the scene as we have come to believe, etc.). On the other hand, some points of contrast may also speak to us more positively and even prophetically: e.g., in the preacher's willingness to speak of every person's mortality when a long life-expectancy could not be presumed.

Those who would prepare and deliver one are reminded here that the children's sermon is not simply a story. Though addressed to children, it is still a sermon, and the preacher—although Hill happily speaks of how engaging stories are—does not confuse sermon and story for a moment. Moreover, like any other sermon, it needs to be prepared, written in advance, and carefully thought out. No mere chat, it aims at theological instruction, and indeed, one will find here a raft of sixteen sermons that lend no basis to the charge that children's sermons amount to a dumbing down of the gospel. No, if anything, these sermons will remind us that our ancestors were no mental slouches, and whatever doctrinal progress we think the church has since made seems pretty meager compared to the abiding, eternal truths that are spoken here.

While the didactic tone of the sermons themselves will be readily enough apparent, there is also a sense in which, where the teaching of preaching is concerned, this short book and these sermons offer a service the author almost certainly did not intend. As the teaching of preaching today shifts (for the sake of practical repetition) toward the study of and training in shorter forms—"Can you state the Gospel in but a single word or short sentence?"—this little book (even where it barely escapes the sphere of mere morals) amounts to a worthwhile object of study for preachers, inviting critical discernment and contextual differentiation, to be sure, but demonstrating far greater potential. For instance, how many four- or five-point children's sermons have you heard lately? The late 19th c. preacher, of course, may well have more readily commanded the attention and respect of his juvenile listeners than informal preachers do today, who seem more determined to slip out from under the mantel of authority than to grow into it and wear it well; nevertheless, here the author readily invites the children to disregard the minister for the sake of remembering that the church is God's house, the Bible is God's book, and all the duties they are expected to perform are for Jesus, whose great sacrifice for us makes it so much easier for us to work for him. Also startling and fresh is the suggestion—when Kierkegaard (who said something similar) had not yet reached the English-speaking world, and Bonhoeffer who quoted him was not yet on the scene—that the Bible may be read as God's love letter to the reader.

Lastly, this unassuming volume stands as a reminder that Christian faith and life, which we regard and feel acutely as counter-cultural today, were likewise counter-cultural when these sermons were penned and shared with the "boys and girls" of Fayetteville, NY, in the early 1880s. In the reference to Moody's story of the half-mile sermon preached by the man who merely carried his Bible with him to church through a tough neighborhood every Sunday, and in the unaffected earnest tone of the series as a whole, there is something about this volume—no mere sentimentality or nostalgia—that makes the case for its resurrection at this time, as a counterpoint to the insufferable, unrelenting irony of the age, as a witness to the strange beauty of the kingdom of God among us, as the lovely fragrance of the gospel that wafts abroad when, in a pinched and selfish world, an unexpected act of unselfishness, an act of grace such as we see in the self-sacrifice of Jesus for our salvation, is witnessed, recognized, and celebrated as the great redeeming expression of God's love for his creation.

—TMS
DUBUQUE, IA
March, 2018

Preface

THE aim of this little book is to show that any minister can give, and that all ought to give, the children of his congregation a portion of the service of worship on the Sabbath.

The writer has been at some pains to ascertain the probable number of ministers who make "five-minute sermons" a regular part of their programme, and finds that there are probably not over two hundred in this country. To increase this number is the aim of this little volume.

The selection of sermons is printed just as they were written and delivered. No claim for special excellence is put forward in printing these sermonettes; the idea being simply this:—that an ordinary country pastor, with no special adaptation to talking to children, seeing that the "children's sermon" idea was a good one, adopted it, and has abundant testimony that it is successful and productive of blessed results. Believing that a like blessing will attend like efforts by others, he sends out these pages with a prayer for that end.

—JCH
Fayetteville, NY
January, 1882

THE CHILDREN'S SERMON

THE CHILDREN'S SERMON

I. Who Started It?

IT may be well to put on record a few items in reference to the history of the movement. The sermons of Dr. Newton, of Philadelphia, to children, have been long and well known. So also have been the "sermons to children," of others. But these were sermons that were designed to be the only sermon in the service. The "Five-minute Sermon" is another thing. We do not know who was the first to venture on this innovation in preaching two sermons at one service. From all that can be learned by the writer, the idea had its rise in Great Britain and the United States about the same time. The first American contribution to the literature of the subject was made by the Rev. J. G. Merrill, of Davenport, Iowa, who published "Twenty-five Sermons to Children," in 1878. This he followed with a larger volume in the course of two years. The Rev. Alexander McLeod, D. D., of Birkenhead, England, at the meeting of the Presbyterian Alliance, in Philadelphia, October, 1880, read a very full paper on the children's portion in public worship. For nearly a year "The Christian at Work" has published weekly a "Five-minute Sermon to Children," by a Brooklyn pastor. The attention of ministers having been directed to the subject in these various ways, gradually a few began the experiment, and the writer has yet to hear of one who has begun and who has failed to continue the practice.

II. What Is It?

1. It is a sermon.
2. It is a sermon to children.
3. It is a sermon five minutes long, to children.

It must be a sermon, not merely a story. If it is a story, there is more prospect of the incidents of the story being the prominent thing than the truth. There is something in the name of the thing that goes a long way towards arresting the attention of the children. It is a sermon to them specially. They rouse themselves to listen, and in time they will pride themselves on being able to tell what the sermon was about.

It is a sermon to children. We must use the greatest care in selecting words, especially if we have not been accustomed to make public addresses to children. Short words and familiar phrases they like to hear. If we use large and unusual words in the sermon, which they cannot understand, they make up their minds that it is a misnomer to call it a children's sermon.

III. *Cui Bono?*

Should not the children listen to the longer sermon? Of course, but it is too long for children, and they forget whole of it unless there is some particular part of it to which their special attention is called. Since their attention has not been specially aroused by the sermon, they are not in the best state for receiving what is offered to them. If you ran give them a little sermon all to themselves, they come to church expecting it; they watch for it; they listen to it; they go home and talk over it, and write to their friends at a distance about it. But will it not get them into the habit of neglecting to listen to the other sermon? What if it does? Have they not received their portion? and, if they are listless during the rest of the service, they have not come in vain if they keep quiet. But they do not increase in listlessness. If we can secure their attention for the five-minute sermon, we have begun to train them to listen to the thirty-minute discourse, and eventually they may be able to stand forty-five minutes, or even an hour on an emergency.

The fact is that the average hearer does not carry away much more than five minutes of the longer sermon from the average minister. If we can give the children, all to themselves, as large a slice as the parents generally take to themselves, we are doing all that we can reasonably expect to accomplish.

The grand aim is to give the children to understand that they constitute a very essential part of the church. They have in many quarters grown up with the idea. that the Sunday-school is church." This idea has been productive of great evils, and especially in the absence of children from the public worship of God and the Lord's Supper. If we call the Sunday-school the "children's church,' then the parents regard the church as their Sunday-school, and the results are that the adults are not in the Sunday-school nor the Children in the church.

The church is made up of believers *and their children.* That which we call the Sunday-school is the assembly of the church for the study of God's word. Hence the same persons should be in each. The work of the church at study cannot be done in the assembly for worship; and while the Sunday-school is a service of worship, it cannot take the place of the great congregation for children any more than it can for parents.

The children's sermon increases the attendance of the children on the services for worship. This is the universal experience. In my own congregation the attendance of children has increased in six months from ten or fifteen to between forty and sixty.

It is relished by adults as well as by the children. There is no doubt but that most ministers preach over the heads of the larger part of their congregations. What the people want is not a display of learning so much as the results of learning simplified. If all our sermons were written down to the comprehension of our boys and girls from twelve to eighteen, that part of our congregations between eighteen and eighty would understand us a good deal better than they now do.

IV. How Is It Done?

It is a sermon. Then take a text, and write the sermon. If you are an extemporaneous preacher, beware. It is a five-minute sermon, and it is to children. Write it, and either read it or deliver it verbatim.

Prepare for it as you would for any other sermon. Use the same variety in structure as you do in your other sermons. But write it, because, if it is over five minutes you will be too long, and if you do not write it you will be apt to make it longer.

Write it, because you then have time to select words that will be better suited to a children's sermon than they would be did you leave their selection until you were on your feet.

Be on the outlook all the time for matter. Look through the children's papers and children's departments of our family papers for illustrations and suggestions as to subjects. Read Dr. Newton's sermons and get his spirit.

Read your sermons to your own children before you preach them, and if you have no children borrow a few from your elders or neighbors, and practice on them. Question them as to the subject, and you will soon learn how to put things so that they will arrest and hold the attention of the children in your congregation.

V. How Begin?

Tell your elders or deacons about it, and they will rejoice. Then tell it to the church, and there will be joy in all the homes. Tell it to the Sunday-school, and there will be waves of smiles and dimples all over the room.

Tell them that on the next Sunday you are going to begin to preach five-minute sermons to children, specially to them, and that after this they will be expected at church just as much as their parents. Do not, however, expect to see the house filled next Sunday. It will take weeks before they get the idea clearly, but after it is evident to children and parents that special attention is to be paid to the young people in the service in which they have been so long neglected, then you will begin to see the fruit of your labor. You will hear more about "the children's sermons" than you do about the others. And the children will begin to realize that the church is not merely for the "big folks."

VI. When?

Before the longer prayer is offered is, perhaps, the best time. My programme is this:

    I. Organ.
    II. Doxology.
    III. Invocation.

IV. Reading Psalm.
V. Hymn.
VI. Reading Scriptures—
   usually reading the passage in which occurs the children's text
VII. Children's Sermon.
VIII. Prayer
IX. Chant by choir.
X. Offerings and notices.
XI. Hymn.
XII. Sermon, and the usual closing services.

The prayer after the sermon usually should begin with such petitions as naturally grow out of the sermon; this tends to hold the attention of the children during this part of the worship. As the sermon takes five minutes from the usual services it would be well if the prayers were shortened, so that the whole service would be no longer than usual.

VII. Every Sabbath?

That is the practice of the greater number of those who preach the children's sermon; but if it be not thought best to have such a sermon every Sabbath, it will be better than having none at all to deliver one at regular stated times, as, for example, once in the month.

THE SERMONS

1. Daisies and Buttercups

"Consider the lilies of the field."— Matt 6:28

ALL around us now the roadsides and fields and hills are beautiful with daisies and buttercups. In the Holy Land the variety of flowers that grow wild is very great. The climate is as varied in the short distance of a hundred miles, in that little country, as it is with us in a thousand miles. In the mountain regions of the northern part they have a climate something like that of Syracuse or Buffalo, while at Jericho it is like New Orleans. The consequence is that the fields there have a great variety of flowers. Someone has said that the Holy Land is a little world of itself, since we can find there trees and flowers which commonly grow only in widely separated parts of the world. Our fruit trees can grow there, and all our flowers, so that were you to go there you would not miss much that you see in the fields here.

The fields there are rich in various kinds of lilies. Christ, when he looked over the fields and roadsides covered with such beautiful colors, wishing to teach a lesson to his hearers, asked them to think of these flowers. Were he among us, no doubt he would have said: "Consider the daisies and buttercups: they toil not, neither do they spin, and yet Solomon in all his glory was not arrayed like one of these."

The daisies and buttercups teach us about God. A blade of green grass tells us a good deal about God, but just take one of these little daisies and see how wonderful it is. It is beautiful in form and elegant in material. No man could ever make a daisy. We see imitations of daisies on the girls' hats sometimes, and at a distance they seem to be real, but if you place a real daisy alongside of an imitation one you will see at once which it was that God made.

1. Daisies and Buttercups

I. The great lesson Christ intended us to learn was, *Trust in God*. He was preaching a sermon. His text was, "Take no anxious thought for the morrow," and he points to the flowers. God, he says, cares for the flowers; he gives them beauty; he sends on them rain and sunshine. Why should you fear and be anxious? God, who cares for the daisies and buttercups, the sparrows and robins, will take care of his dear children.

II. The daisies and buttercups teach us a lesson of *Humility*.

One sin into which a great many are very apt to fall is pride of dress. Some people spend more money on make-believe-flowers for a hat or a bonnet than they will give for missions in a whole year. They think that if they can only get something to wear that no one else has, they will be the happiest people in the world; but this is all wrong. Think of the daisies and buttercups. They out-do Solomon in all his glory. They do not worry and fret over dress, for God has provided them with beauties, and yet how simple is the dress! It does not require either rich material or brilliant colors to dress neatly.

III. The daisies and buttercups tell us that *we soon must die.* The flowers soon fade. It will not be many weeks until you may hunt for a daisy and you will not be able to find one. Just as surely are *we* fading. We are not like the oaks and the pines that last for hundreds of years; we are just like these daisies and buttercups, staying only a little while on the earth. The glory of man is as the flower of the field.

Our Saviour is likened to the flowers, but in another way. He is lovely and beautiful and humble. He is "the rose of Sharon and the lily of the valleys." If we think of these flowers and the lessons they teach, we may become like him, lovely, beautiful and humble.

2. Burdock And Thistles

"And other fell among the thorns, and the thorns grew up, and choked it, and it yielded no fruit."
— Mark 4:7

AS daisies and buttercups taught us something suggested by our Lord's words, "Consider the lilies," I think that today we can learn something from burdock and thistles in connection with this text. Whilst The Holy Land has our flowers, it also has our weeds.

The general name given to weeds in the Bible is "thorns and thistles." There are some twenty different Hebrew and Greek words used by the writers of the books of the Bible for these weeds. They were not all thorny or prickly. Some of them were like our common weeds, but in our version of the Bible all go under the name of " thorns and thistles," just as we include all kinds under the general name "weeds."

A sower went out to sow, our Lord says, and some of his seed fell where it was picked up by the birds; some fell among the weeds, but the weeds grew faster than the grain, and the result was that the grain was killed out. When our farmers plant corn they have to keep continually plowing out the weeds. When we plant our gardens we need to keep weeding all the time or we shall have neither flowers nor vegetables. Now let us learn some lessons from weeds.

1. *We find them everywhere.*

The good seed that God sows in our hearts by his word, in the church, or in the Sunday-school or prayer meeting, or in the home at family worship, or in conversation or study—does not all bear fruit. There are weeds in our hearts. As we find weeds in every field, so we find weeds in the heart of every boy and girl, that interfere with the bearing of good fruit.

2. *Weeds are hard to get rid of.*

I have tried to get burdock and thistles out of my lawn by cutting off the top close by

2. Burdock And Thistles

the root, but it does not take long for them to grow again. I find the only way to get rid of them is to "root them out." So with the weeds in our hearts: we can't cut down our bad habits to the root and expect that that will be the end of them. We must hoe them out completely.

3. *One hoeing is not enough.*

I find that after every shower there is a new crop of weeds coming up. The seeds of weeds lie in the soil for years, until a favorable opportunity comes, and then they sprout. And you must not think that because you have gotten rid of one bad thing, or another, that you are free from soul-weeds. The seeds of sin's weeds lie buried in your very soul, and will certainly grow and choke the good seed unless you watch them and fight them.

4. *The weeds come up every year.*

If we make our fields ever so clean we must not think that next year we shall be free from weeds. Our neighbors do not always keep their fields clean, and then in the roads the weeds grow luxuriantly; and the seeds are blown from these fields and *highways* over our gardens and fields by the winds. As long as we are in this world, we shall be in danger of having floating seeds of sin find a resting-place in our souls.

The only thing then for us to do is to be continually weeding and hoeing, watching our souls every day for the weeds of passion, of disobedience, of bad thoughts and bad words. If we ask God to help us to be watchful, he will, by his Spirit, so help us that the weeds will not be allowed to choke out the truth.

3. Snow

"He giveth snow like wool."—Psalm 147:16

TAKING the whole year round, there is perhaps no time when there is so *much fun* for boys and girls as when there is snow on the ground. Last year we had very little snow and no ice, while this year (winter of 1880–81) there is an abundance of both, and the snow and ice are a source of much joy to you all.

As we see so much snow in the winter, and see it every year, we come to regard it as a very common and ordinary thing, and not worth any special attention, except for sleighing and coasting, and building forts and snow men. I wonder how many of you have thought of the snow as coming from God. Snow is the gift of God. Although sometimes it seems to us a great inconvenience, we ought to regard snow as one of God's best gifts.

I. *It is a beautiful.*

Each crystal of snow is a perfect gem of beauty. As the snow falls some day, if you will take a magnifying glass and closely examine a few flakes, you will find that each one is formed on the plan of a six-pointed star. There never was a flake of snow that had seven points or five—never more nor less than six. It is the same in Greenland as it is here, and every flake is perfect and exquisite in beauty. Now it is only God that could make this constant, perfect and abounding beauty. But the snow is not only beautiful in its single flakes: when it has settled in masses on the trees and hills it is beautiful. Although in winter there is not the variety of colors that you can see in summer, yet you can see in the winter mornings and evenings, at sunrise and sunset, beauties that summer can never show you. Like white flakes of wool, God sends down the snow to make the earth beautiful.

2. *It is a useful gift.*

Things may be beautiful but not useful. Now snow is both beautiful and useful. Our text says God gives snow like wool. In Canaan they used only linen and wool for clothing, largely wool. They had great flocks of sheep, from which they obtained the wool, and in using wool for cloth they were able to make it exceedingly white—so white that it must have been almost as white as the snow. Wool was used for clothing, and so God gives the snow for a covering for the earth, as we use woolen garments to keep us warm. The earth needs to be kept warm as well as our bodies. Sometimes there are parts of our fields that do not become covered with the snow in winter, and the consequence is that the grain sown in the fall is killed by the frost. Last spring I remember seeing a wheat field only about half of which was green. On asking the reason, I found that the snow had drifted to one part of the field and had left the other part bare all winter. The part on which there had been snow all winter had been kept warm, and when the sun in the spring melted the snow the wheat was ready to begin to grow. It is practically the same with everything else. The colder the country is the more snow they have to keep the ground from freezing so deeply as to kill the plants and trees.

So you can see how good God is in giving snow, so beautiful and so useful too. We have no flowers in the fields in winter, but you must remember that we have the more flowers in summer because we have the snow in winter.

There is another verse in the Bible about snow and wool that you ought to remember: "Come now, and let us reason together, saith the Lord; though your sins be as scarlet they shall be white as snow; though they be red like crimson they shall be as wool."

Sin is represented in the Bible as dirt—filth, something from which we need to be cleansed. Things that are dirty are easily washed; even things dyed black can be bleached. If you go to the paper mill you will find that they take in all sorts of dirty rags, and when these are bleached they come out white, and after they are washed and ground up and put through the paper machine there comes out the long ribbon of beautiful white paper. But I am told that there is a certain

3. Snow

kind of rag that they can't bleach. It is those rags that are dyed with a peculiar kind of red. All the skill of the chemists has not been able to discover a way by which these crimson or scarlet rags can be bleached. Now look at these words: "though your sins be as scarlet they shall be white as snow; though they be red like crimson they shall be as wool." This is intended to teach us that we cannot wash out the stains that sin has made on our souls. Our souls ought to be like snow, but they are not, on account of our sins. God wants us to learn that it is only the precious blood of Christ that can wash out these crimson stains of sin.

God will not only wash, but will keep you pure. Let your prayer be:

"Lord Jesus, I long to be perfectly whole:
I want thee forever to live in my soul;
Break down every idol, cast out every foe—
Now wash me, and I shall be whiter than snow."

4. Sin

My little children, these things write I unto you, that ye sin not." —1 John 2:1

SIN is the most awful thing in the universe. The first sin was committed in heaven. Angels disobeyed God, and God could not permit sin in heaven, so he drove out the angels that sinned.

Man was created holy and set in the garden of Eden. But man also sinned, Adam and Eve fell, and all of their children have followed them in sinning. The result is that we do not enjoy God as we should. It is on account of sin that we do not naturally love to hear about God and his holy book, or to meet with his people for worship; and it is not the nature of sin to stand still: it grows.

4. Sin

A story is told of a wicked king who called one of his subjects to him and asked him what his trade was. He said he was a blacksmith. "Go home then and make me a chain ten cubits long." He made it and brought it to the king, who told him to go home and make it twenty cubits. Every time the blacksmith finished it, he was required to add ten more cubits to it. At last the poor smith murmured; he had received no wages, and he could no longer carry the chain, it was so heavy. The king told his servants to take the man and bind him with his chain and cast him into the sea.

This was his wages, and this is just what sin does: it makes a chain that grows longer every day, that will only in the end be used to bind us completely and sink us deeper. Sin pays no wages but death. "The wages of sin is death."

Now John wrote part of this letter to the children in order to show them how they might not sin. John wrote to show us how God hates sin; and to show us that sin not only makes us unhappy but that it will prevent us from enjoying God. The Bible was written for this; and what I wish to impress on you this morning is this, that we can't overcome sin unless we use God's word.

David said, "Thy word have I hid in my heart, that I might not sin against thee." He meant that he had learnt God's law, his promises and precepts, and that when he remembered these they kept him from sinning. If our hearts are full of the word, we shall be prevented from sinning.

You know how our Lord himself overcame Satan when he was tempted. Every temptation he resisted by quoting a verse of Scripture. When we have the example of David and of our Lord, and these words of our text, we can surely see that if we follow their example we shall be able to overcome also.

When you are tempted to sin think of what God says about it: "The wages of sin is death," and ask yourself, as Joseph did, "How can I do this great wickedness and sin against God?"

5. Sin Forgiven

"Blessed is he whose transgression is forgiven,
whose sin is covered."—Psalm 32:1

WE all know that sin is of such a nature that we would be very glad to get rid of it—to get rid of everything that is sinful and away from everybody that sins. If there were nothing bad in the world, then we should have heaven on earth. But as long as we live we shall have to be troubled by sin and its consequence, both in ourselves and from others. Now if you can imagine what this world would be were there nothing bad in it, then you will have an idea of what the word *blessed* means. It is a word we use very often. It does not mean merely happy; people may be happy and not blessed. People are often happy in sin. Blessedness is a happiness that is the result of the putting away of sin. We might call it religious happiness. Now the text speaks of the man who is blessed, and gives the reason for it. His transgression is forgiven and his sin is covered. Transgression and sin mean about the same thing.

Transgression is the same as trespassing. For instance, if a man has a fine lot of grapes on his vines and some boys climb over his fence to find out if they are ripe, we call that trespassing; it is going where they have no business to go. That is what sin is. God has told us what we ought to do, and what we ought not to do. He has put a fence around us and he says, "You keep inside of this fence; all outside is Satan's world. If you go outside you are trespassing; it is wrong. Stay on this side of the fence and you will do right. Go over and you will do wrong."

Sin is about the same thing; it means something that is uneven or crooked. God tells us how to walk—straight forward in the line marked out by the Bible; but when we get off the line, we make a crooked path.

5. Sin Forgiven

Let me illustrate this by a little story. Two boys had crossed a field on their way to school one day after the first snow in winter. After they had crossed the field, they looked back and saw that one path was very straight and the other was very crooked. The one who made the crooked path said to the other: "How comes it that your path is so straight and mine so crooked?" "Why," said he, "I just kept my eye on the old tree at the school-house door, and walked straight to it." Now if we could only see the tracks we make by our lives, we would see that instead of being very straight, they are zig-zag, crooked, and every way. This is the only way they can be if we do not keep our eye on our Saviour.

Now, then, what is to be done with us when we trespass—when we go where we ought not, or do what we ought not? God says the soul that sinneth, it shall die. That is an awful thing. But God so loved the world that he gave his only begotten Son that whosoever believeth in him should not perish, but have everlasting life. God does not want those that sin to die, and so he offers to forgive trespasses and to cover up sin.

This means, that if you will believe what God says about his Son Jesus, and ask him to forgive you, he will not think any more of your disobedience—of your trespasses; he will forgive you, or send away your transgression—he will send it away out of his sight, and he will cover your sin. The crooked tracks your sins have made will be covered up so that he cannot see them.

But you must understand that before God can forgive your transgressions and cover your sins you must repent of what you have done; you must be sorry for sin, because it has made God sorry; and you must give it up, turn away from it, leave it forever.

And lastly, remember that God forgives and covers the sins only of those who ask him to do it when they are truly sorry for these sins.

There are some things God gives to everybody without asking for them, as the air, and light; but you can only get forgiveness by asking for it.

If you ask him he will not refuse. He will send his Spirit to tell you that you are one of

5. Sin Forgiven

God's children, and to make you, not merely happy, but blessed.

Only in this way can you receive the blessing.

6. Prayer

"Pray to thy Father." — Matt. 5:6.

I DO not suppose that there is a child in this congregation who has not been taught at some time to say its prayers, and some of you just keep "saying your prayers" and never pray.

There is a great difference between praying and saying prayers. I remember once seeing a curious little thing that was brought from India by a missionary. It looked very much like one of those machines the boys make for a rattle, where you have a piece of wood twirled on a handle, and as you twirl it, it makes a fearful racket. Now this rattle had a little drawer in one side of it, and in the drawer there was a piece of paper on which were written very curious characters. The missionary told me that this was a praying machine. The Hindu wrote his prayer on the little slip of paper and then put it into the little drawer and began whirling it by the handle, and every time it turned around he supposed he said a prayer, and that the longer he turned the machine the more he was likely to receive the blessing he desired from God.

Do not we offer just the same kind of machine prayers? A great many simply repeat a prayer, and when they have done that, they think they have performed their duty.

These machine prayers were very much in fashion among the Jews when Christ lived, and he warned people against the sin. You remember he said: "Use not vain repetitions as the heathen do, for they think they shall be heard much speaking." When you want something from your mother you go to her at once and ask for it, and you know that if it is right and your mother is able to give it to you, she will do so. That is just what prayer is. It is asking for what you want from one who is able to give it, and with the belief that you will get it. As we

THE CHILDREN'S SERMON

cannot serve God without knowing what he wants us to do, and as we cannot have the pardon of our sins without asking for it, and as we cannot obey him without his help, and as we cannot obtain that help without asking for it, it follows that those who only make machine prayers and never really pray must have a very hard time of it in trying to be good. You can only be good by God's help, and you can only have that help by asking for it.

It is a very easy thing to some people to be good. You know that; you know some of your companions whom you consider very good, and you say to yourself: "I have such a hard time of it; it's so hard to be good, and there's this one and that one—it seems to come easy to them."

Why is it so? It is this: they ask God for help, and the more accustomed they are to ask him, the more joyous is the work. There is a pump over at the manse that is not very much in use. It had not been in use for some months; the leather valves became very hard and dry, and we could get no water by pumping. One day a workman took it to pieces and soaked the leathers, and then

6. Prayer

poured some water into the pump, and soon the water came. But, as soon as we were done pumping, it ran down again, and the only way we can get water out of that pump is by pouring water down. There is another pump that is in use every day, and a great many times a day, and if we want water there, all we have to do is simply to give a few strokes of the handle and up comes the water at once. Why? because it is in constant use. Now this illustrates prayer and its effects on our hearts and lives. Prayer is the pump by which supplies of God's help are pumped into our souls, and if the pump is dry, our souls are dry, and if we want any of God's help, we may have to go to work and thaw out frozen pipes and pour hot water down, and all that sort of thing, before we can get anything; but if the pump of prayer is in constant use, we receive the blessing we want at once.

If you are not in the habit of prayer, you have a very miserable, dry time of it. You know you ought to pray to God. It is not so much where you pray, or when you pray, but that you do pray. The Jews had little rooms in their gardens and on the tops of their houses for praying in. This was well; a quiet place helps prayer, but this is not necessary. You can pray walking along the street, in school, at play, morning, noon, night, any time, anywhere.

Ask God for just what you want. Tell him your troubles and your temptations, and he will supply all you need for the sake of his Son, our Lord Jesus.

7. Walking with God

"Enoch walked with God." — Gen. 5:24

WHEN we see two boys or two girls always walking with each other we know that they must be very close friends; we know that they must love each other. We know that if they hated each other they would keep away from each other's company. That is just what is meant by "walking with God." We find such expressions as, "Walk worthy of your calling;" "Walk as children of the light;" and then our text. In these verses the *walk* means the whole life, so that if we live with God we walk with God.

I. Enoch lived with God; he made God his constant companion. You can do the same. You must remember that God is not so far away that you cannot get near him or he get near to you. The fact is, God can be as close to you as your friend who walks along the street with you. God can just as really walk with you as your friends can.

2. If you can walk with God, you can of course talk with him and he can talk with you. When you are walking along the street with your friends you are generally talking. In fact, wherever we see people together we generally find them talking to each other. So in your walk with God. You can talk to him in prayer, and in your thoughts. Of courses you can't see him, but he is just as real as your companion on the street, and will just as really hear you speak. God, who made our ears, can hear as well as we, and God talks to you although you cannot hear his voice. He puts thoughts into your mind; he tells you what is right, and warns against what is wrong.

3. Now God cannot walk with you unless there is friendship. Those who are not friends cannot walk together. "How can two walk together except they be agreed?" Now, by nature, you don't like God; you don't love him as you do your parents. So, in order to have you love him, he pardons your sins, for

7. Walking with God

he cannot walk with those who are not sorry for sin and so he makes you sorry, and then you ask him to forgive you. If you love to sin you cannot have friendship for God; so if you are to walk with God, you must hate sin and forsake it.

4. Walking with God does not mean meeting him occasionally by chance. We sometimes meet a friend on the street and walk with him a little way, and then we may not see him for a week and more; that is not the kind of walking Enoch did with God; his walking was continual. He did not walk with God one day and with Satan the next, but he walked with God all the time. So must we.

5. If we walk with God like Enoch we shall become like God. Enoch became like God, and he was perhaps the best man that lived before the flood; so good that God did not allow him to die in the usual way, but took him out of the world, in some way, direct to heaven.

Friends among boys and girls pick up each other's habits—sometimes good, and sometimes bad; so, if we walk with God, we can't help but pick up godly habits. We shall think as he thinks; we shall love what he loves; we shall hate what he hates; we shall also love to do what God asks us to do, and we shall grow so much like him, and so loving to him, that we shall never leave his side.

8. The Lamp

"Thy word is a lamp unto my feet."— Psalm 119:105

YOU will remember that not long ago our little children's sermon was on walking with God. This text is one of the same kind. We walk a great deal; we could do very little unless we walked. If we could not walk, we should be almost helpless. Walking, then, is a very important thing. In order to walk, God has given us feet of such a shape that we can stand upright upon them, and walk upright. Our feet are almost as wonderful as our hands. Our feet, however, are not made for rough roads, as a horse's foot or a dog's foot is. These are protected so that they are not liable to be cut or injured by the uneven surface on which they may go. Our feet were designed for walking on smooth places. If your toes get into a hole the result is most likely to be you fall.

Now unless we are very sure that we know the walk on which we are, we naturally look at it to see that we avoid anything that may cause us to fall. Often, when we think everything is right, we are deceived. In our village just now, in our board side-walks there are a great many broken and loose planks; these are so dangerous that in walking over them you need to be very cautious, for you don't know at what moment you may be tripped. But when you come to the asphalt walk; you then feel more secure and take firmer steps. In daylight you have very little trouble, but at night there is. danger in walking over a board side-walk; so that at night you need to have a light. The best light is one that you can carry in your hand, so that it will shine down near your feet, in order that you may see where you are going. Now David says, in our text, that God's word is like a light of this kind — a hand-lantern. "Thy word is a lamp unto my feet." He means that if he did not have God's word to show him how to live, what to do, how to love, praise and serve God, he would

8. The Lamp

be the same as a man wandering around whilst trying to find his way on a dark night. The Bible should be used by every one as his lamp. There is no way by which we can see the right path except by this lamp, which tells us what to do and what to avoid. But a lantern will not show the way unless we use it, and before it is of any use it must be filled with oil and lighted.

Just so is it with the Bible. The book itself, as a book, is of no use, no matter how nicely it may be bound, no matter how beautiful the paper may be. If it is not used it is of no value.

Every day in walking you need to watch your feet, to see that you do not trip; so every day you need to watch the feet of your soul.

Your whole life ought to be a continual watching, lest you do anything that displeases God. As Satan places many traps in your way, like those dangerous, loose planks in our side-walks, you need to be very careful. But if you use God's word, by studying it and storing it in your mind, so that it will be at hand when you want it, you will not be in danger.

You know some very good people, and you often wish you could be as good as they are. The secret of their goodness is their use of God's word. If you use it as they do you will become better in your life, for God will be with you and help you to avoid the dangerous places. They will be seen by the light of the lamp of his word.

9. A Boy Who Walked With God

2 Chron. 34:1-4

JOSIAH was the best king the Hebrews had, although not the greatest; but it is better to be good than to be great. He became king when he was only eight years old, and he reigned in Jerusalem for thirty-one years.

We have seen in these short sermons how a man walked with God—Enoch; and in the last one how we are to walk—with God's word as our lantern. This morning I have thought that perhaps some of you boys and girls might say: "Well, all that is for big folks: we can't do what Enoch did: he was a man; and then we can't understand much of the Bible anyway."

Now, as some you are very apt to think this way, and I know boys who say that, I wish this morning to let you know about king Josiah.

Josiah was a boy when he became king. While he was yet young he began to seek after God, and he walked in the ways of David his father, and inclined neither to the right hand nor to the left. What is said of Josiah is better than can be said of David—"he turned neither to the right hand nor to the left." This is a wonderful record to leave, and we must accept it as true.

I want you to feel that the same thing is possible for each of you. Josiah was just like you. He was a boy who loved fun just as much as you do, but he saw that walking with God and turning neither to the right hand nor to the left would not prevent him from enjoying himself. This is the point at which so many boys and girls, and old folks too, make a very great mistake. They think that if they were to begin to walk with God they must give up their enjoyments. This is all wrong, for the fact is, that it is only those who do walk with God that know how to enjoy themselves properly. If Josiah had said to himself, "I will wait until I am a man and then think about religion," the chances are

9. A Boy Who Walked with God

that he would never have walked with God at all. It is the same with you. If you don't begin to walk with God while you are young you will probably never do it.

Away off in the Rocky Mountains are two little springs, very near each other, and out of each runs a little stream of water. They are so near each other that with very little trouble you could change the course of one into the other; but as they flow out of their pools the one little brook goes off to the east, while the other goes to the west. As they flow on they gain in size, and they flow on and on, through valleys and plains, each one joined by a thousand other streams, until at last one empties into the Gulf of Mexico, as the Mississippi; and the other little brook of the mountains we find emptying into the Pacific Ocean as the Columbia River. Two brothers or sisters begin life like these two mountain streams; the one begins to walk with God and the other does not. Their lives flow on in opposite directions, the distance widening all the time, until their souls are far apart as the mouths of the Mississippi and the Columbia Rivers. You can easily change your course while you are young, but when you are older it is well nigh an impossibility, and on account of its difficulty very few attempt it.

Take Josiah, then, as an example. If he, a king, could walk with God, surrounded by all the temptations of wicked men at his court (and the last king had a great many wicked men around him)—if he, amid all these temptations, could walk with God and turn not to the right hand nor to the left, it is possible for you to do the same.

10. "Not your own."

"Ye are not your own; for ye are bought with a price."—1Cor 6:19-20

WHEN you buy a thing and pay for it you call it your own. God considers what he has bought and paid for as his own. You know what a slave is. He is a man who has been bought and paid for to be a servant, and he is required to work for his master as long as he lives, without receiving what we call wages, because he has been bought and paid for by his master. All his time belongs to his master, because he has paid for it. He considers that he owns the whole of the man—his hands and feet and mind. We have no slaves now in our country, but that is the way in which slaves are regarded by their owners.

They are not their own.

A man who is not a slave thinks he is his own. He has a right to the use of his own hands and feet and mind. Instead of having to work for one master, whether he is treated well or not, a free man can work for whom he pleases. He feels that his body is his own, and that he can do as he wishes. This is all true, in a certain sense, but Paul in our text says it is not true of believers in the Lord Jesus Christ. He tells them that they are not their own—"Ye are not your own," for God has bought you with a price.

The price that God paid for you was the life of his holy Son Jesus.

Believers, then, have no right to their bodies, to use them only for their own advantage. You have been bought by God, and hence he owns you, just as really as a slave is owned by his master. So we find Paul calling himself, not a mere servant of Christ, but a slave of Christ, one who has been bought and paid for.

We must, then, yield our members to the service of God if we are not our own.

1. *Your hands* must be God's. You must then see that you do not let Satan use your

10. "Not your own"

hands as though they were his. You can do a great many bad things with your hands. Remember, then, that your hands are God's—"not your own;" and let them do only those things that will be for God's glory.

2. *Your feet* are God's, too, remember. You must not let them do Satan's work. Do not let them carry you away from the right path.

3. *Your eyes* are God's. Keep your eyes then at work for him. You can see a great deal through your eyes. Eve began to sin through her eyes. Turn your eyes away from whatever would lead you to sin.

4. *Your ears* are not your own. Take heed then what you hear. It is through the eye and the ear that most of the evil enters our souls. Do not listen then to anything that you know is wrong.

5. So, also, *your tongue* is not your own. The tongue is the one member of our bodies that is most apt to cause us to sin, and it therefore requires most care. If before you speak you could just remember that your tongue is God's, and not your own, then you would not say so many bad things; you would not use so many angry, unkind words; you

would not cause trouble by your thoughtless words.

If you remember that you are not your own: that your hands and feet, and eyes and ears, and tongue and heart, are God's, then you will be a slave of Christ, like Paul; but in that service you will have a liberty that the slaves of sin and Satan know nothing about.

11. Who Is On The Lord's Side?

Exodus 32:26

THE children of Israel had made a golden calf and were worshiping it as though it were God. This, of course, was very displeasing to God, who had only a little while before saved them from the Egyptians. And now, while Moses was away from them in Mount Sinai, to receive the Law of God, they forgot all about what God had done for them. They made an idol and were worshiping it. When Moses saw this he was very much provoked. Thinking that perhaps some of them had not forgotten God, he went off to one side and called out: "Who is on the Lord's side? Come to me!"

THE CHILDREN'S SERMON

We are always "taking sides." Sometimes, when two boys quarrel, some of those around will be on the side of one, and some on the side of the other. In the last election everybody took sides. Some were Republicans and some were Democrats. It was sometimes hard to tell what side a man was going to vote on. Sometimes there would be a man who had not decided on which side he would go. But this question, "Who is on the Lord's side?" is one on which there must be a decision. When Moses wanted those who were on the Lord's side to show themselves, he said: "Come to me." Every one of the Israelites should have gone over to Moses, but not all did.

I. Those who did not go on the Lord's side, could give no good reason for not doing it. The golden calf had done nothing for them, while God had done much. Now, you are just like the children of Israel; you are either worshiping an idol or you are worshiping God. You are doing one or the other. You are either on the Lord's side, or against him. You know on which side you ought to be.

11. Who Is On the Lord's Side?

II. There is great danger to you if you do not come on the Lord's side. There were three thousand men killed that day, because they did not come over on the Lord's side. And a similar evil will come upon every one who refuses to be on the Lord's side. If you are not on the Lord's side, you will never be allowed by God to enjoy the blessings which he gives only to those who are on his side.

III. Your duty is to decide to be on the Lord's side at once. It is not merely a duty, but a privilege, and it will be to your honor and advantage; but, above all it will be for God's glory.

IV. The way to show that you are on the Lord's side is to separate yourself from sinful things, sinful companionships, sinful words, sinful thoughts. But you cannot do this without God's help. You know you have often tried to be good, but you have found that somehow you could not. The trouble has been that you forgot that God could help you.

Ask God, then, to help you to show that you are on his side. Ask him to give you his Holy Spirit, and then you will be filled with something that will not allow sin to be in your mind. Join yourself with God's people;

be with them in the church, in the Sabbath-school, and in the prayer meeting. Ask God to help you, and then he will *keep* you on his side.

12. Christ's Invitation to His Supper

"Suffer the little children, and forbid them not, to come unto me." — Matt. 19:14

YOU have heard these words very often; so often that you may think you know what they mean. I hope you do, and this morning I wish to have you *think* about the meaning, and then see if you will not *do* what they mean.

The words were spoken by Jesus. He very often said, "Come unto me." He said, "Come unto me all ye that labor." In fact, the whole gospel in one word is, "Come."

Now I know that you children very often have the idea that religion, the church, and all these things, are for older people only;

THE CHILDREN'S SERMON

and that before you can be religious and come to Christ and to the Lord's Supper you must be much older than you are. This is a great mistake. For Christ says: "Suffer the little children to come unto me."

There was a crowd around Jesus; there were a good many mothers there—some carrying their babies in their arms, and some leading their children by the hand. There were little children, young children and infants. This description means children from a year old up to twelve or thirteen. These mothers brought their children to Jesus, because they knew that he would be glad to bless them. They knew that if they were brought to Jesus once while young they would never forget it, and would be his all their lives.

Now Jesus is just the same today in heaven that he was while on the earth. If he wished the children to come to him then, he wishes them to come to him now. We come to him when we eat and drink at his table, to show him that we love him.

Do not think that you must know a great deal before you come to the Lord's table. Of course, you do not know as much as your

12. Christ's Invitation to His Supper

parents; it is not necessary that you should. It is not necessary that you should know all the doctrines of the church and be able to explain them. There are a great many older people who do not know all the doctrines, nor can they explain them, and yet they have a perfect right to come to the Lord's table.

All who believe that they love Jesus have a right to come to his table, and it makes no difference how old they are, or how much they know.

Sometimes children as young as four years have been known to be qualified to come to the Lord's table. It is not necessary for you to be able to answer a great many puzzling questions, that many suppose are asked in what is called the "examination." All that the session members do is to have a little talk with you to find out whether you love Jesus as your own precious Saviour; whether, knowing that you are sinful, you have asked God for Jesus' sake to pardon you; whether you are trying, with God's help, to obey him and to become more like Jesus every day.

If you can say that you do love Jesus, that you have asked God for the pardon of your sins and for help to obey him, and if your life, so far as known, shows that you answer truly, then you will be gladly welcomed to the Lord's table.

This is all that we can consistently ask of you.

Don't think you are too young to come to the Lord's table. Many of the most eminent men in the Christian church were admitted to the Lord's table when very young— Polycarp at nine years of age; Matthew Henry, the great commentator, at eleven; the great theologian, Jonathan Edwards, at seven; Dr. Isaac Watts, the writer of so many hymns, at nine. Scores could be named who afterwards became useful Christian men and women, who were received at like early ages.

There are many of you who are already members of the church by baptism. You have been taught the Catechism; you can read God's word; you have been, and are, taught to pray, to abhor sin, to fear God, and obey the Lord Jesus Christ. Many of you are really pious children. To those of you who are thus, as children, performing the duties of Christians, and are old enough to know what the Lord's Supper means—and you may

12. Christ's Invitation to His Supper

know that very young—I now say that it is your duty and your privilege to come to the Lord's table.

Think over these words of our Lord: "Suffer the little children to come unto me," and see if you do not find a new meaning in them today.

13. The Lord's Supper

"This do in remembrance of me."—Luke 22:19

EVERY boy knows something about the Fourth of July. We call it Independence Day. It is a celebration of the event by which this country became free and independent. It is a remembrance every year of the beginning of our present prosperity and happiness. In every country there is some day that is celebrated in the same way; for instance, in Canada they have the first of July, which is called by them "Dominion Day"— that is, the day on which the various separate provinces belonging to England became consolidated into one grand dominion. In England they celebrate the birthday of Queen Victoria, the 24th of May. These days are celebrated by all

13. The Lord's Supper

the people just as we celebrate the Fourth of July.

The Hebrews had a day that was just the same as our Independence Day. It was the day that commemorated their freedom as a nation—their deliverance from the slavery of Egypt; and that day is celebrated by them every year even till today. It keeps them in constant remembrance of the mercy of God towards them as a nation. The way in which they used to celebrate that day is very different from the way in which we celebrate our Fourth of July. God told them what they were to do. They were to have a supper, specially prepared for each family by themselves. It was called the Passover supper. There was a certain kind of bread and vegetables that they were to eat, and they always remembered to do it. The priests killed the lamb that was to be eaten, and they were very careful to do exactly as God had commanded them to do.

One night, as they were celebrating this national holiday at Jerusalem, there was a remarkable company of men gathered in an upper chamber in Jerusalem. They were doing the same things that the other two or

THE CHILDREN'S SERMON

three millions of people were doing in the city. These men were from Galilee, and as they were about finishing the meal, one of them interrupted the usual customs, and in a very solemn way told the others of a new supper that they were to have forever after that. He told them that the Old Testament was ended and that a New Testament had begun. He told them that the blood of the lamb that had been killed and sprinkled for these fifteen centuries was only intended to remind them that God would at some time send his Lamb to be slain, and that *he* was the Lamb of God. He took bread in his hand and said, This bread is *my* body—broken — given — for you. Taking also a cup of wine he said, This wine is my blood—shed for you. As often as you eat bread and drink wine, as I have shown you here, you will declare the fact that I have died for the remission, for the pardon, of sins, and that through my blood only is there forgiveness. He told them that by doing as they had done that night, until he would come to earth again, they would keep alive the remembrance of his death and love.

13. The Lord's Supper

Now all of you, children, who are here this morning have seen this service before. We are to engage in it today, in obedience to Christ; we are going to do the same today that Christ's people have done for nearly two thousand years. I wish you today to be very attentive to what is done, for the Lord's Supper was intended by our Lord as a children's sermon, to be preached by every minister of his gospel. If there are some things that you do not understand, when you go home ask your parents about them, and they will be glad to tell you.

14. Working for Jesus

"Lord, what wilt thou have me to do?"— Acts 9:6

JESUS wants us to do something for him. Paul saw that just as soon as he was converted; and each one of you, children, must see that Jesus wants you to do something for him, just as really as he wanted Paul to do something for him.

Are you doing anything for Jesus? Just think and see if you are really doing anything for Jesus. I am afraid that many of you will find that you are doing nothing.

There is a very celebrated picture in Europe that represents Jesus dying on the cross. It is a picture that is so real that it makes you almost think you actually see the real Jesus in his great suffering. It is a picture before which a great many linger a

14. Working for Jesus

long time, and so deep is the impression made that often the most careless visitor weeps before it. Upon the frame of the picture is a card on which is written a question that brings the scene home to each heart. The question is this: "I did this for thee: what art thou doing for me?" A great many look at Christ and love him, and are made very sorry when they think of how cruelly he suffered; but there they stop. They just think of what Christ did for them, and never think that they ought to do something for Christ.

Now notice that Paul's question was not, "Lord, what wilt thou have *us* do?" It was, "What wilt thou have ME to do?" We have a church here, and we are all engaged in the work of the church, but a great many do not take any active part in it. They think the question has *us* in it instead of *me*. Now each one of you little boys and girls has a part of the Lord's work to do, just the same as older people have. There is something for even children to do, and no one of you will be excused by the Lord from doing your share of his work.

There is something that you can do that no one else can do, and if you do not do it, it is left undone forever.

You may ask me, what is there that I can do for Jesus? There are thousands of little things you can do; let me tell you of a few that will do a great deal of good.

1. One is, be kindly affectionate, one to another. Be kind; speak kindly; or, to put it in another way, don't get angry; don't speak cross words; don't get "the sulks." I know that it is sometimes very hard to do this, but if you will remember that it is for Jesus that you do it, you will find it easier.

2. *Another thing is, be generous.* Remember that it is more blessed to give than to receive. Now if you give for Jesus, you will be still more blest. If you can overcome your selfish disposition, you are doing something for Jesus. And this will be something that will do a great amount of good in the world. The world is full of selfishness. If anyone displays an unselfish spirit, it is like the opening of a bottle of delightful perfume. Everyone around feels the influence of such a life.

14. Working for Jesus

3. *Another thing, study for Jesus.* I mean not only the Bible lessons, but your day-school lessons. It is a part of your work for Jesus to learn your lessons well. The more knowledge you have, the better you will be able to serve Jesus when you get older.

4. Look upon all the little duties of the school and the home as a part of your work for Jesus.

Remember that it is FOR JESUS. We are told to do everything in his name, and that means the same as doing it for him. If we find some things hard to do; if you have the same thing to do over and over again every day and get tired of it; if you remember that it is for Jesus, it will make a great difference. Remember, then, to do everything for Jesus.

This, you see, will help you to tell what you ought to do. If you are asked to do something, or if you want to do something that you are not just sure is right, ask yourself: "Can I do this for Jesus?" If you cannot do it for him, do not do it at all. Thus your whole life will be his.

15. Going to Church

"I was glad when they said unto me, Let us go into the house of the Lord."—Psalm 122:1

IT was David that said this. He was glad when the time came to go to church. This is the way in which everyone should feel in reference to the church. God's people have always had places or houses in which they gathered to worship him regularly, and he has always blessed them when they met together in his name. Now a great many think it is a task, a hardship, to come to church. Instead of saying, "I was glad when they said unto me, Let us go into the house of the Lord," they say, "I don't care much about going to church; the sermons are so long and so dry, and the minister reads such

15. Going to Church

long chapters, I always feel very tired; and I don't like to go to church anyway."

There are a great many boys and girls that feel just that way. I know how they feel. I was once a boy, and used to like to stay at home instead of going to church. The trouble with boys and girls is that they think that the church is a meeting from which people can stay away if they choose. They see that a good many people stay at home on Sunday and from the prayer-meeting, and they get the idea that there is no obligation on them or on anyone else to attend. But if anyone stays away from God's house without good reason, he is doing very wrong.

We come to church not simply to hear the minister preach. His sermons are a small part of the whole service. I want you to remember that churches are not merely for men to preach in, but that they are for God's people to gather in to hear his word read, and to sing his praise and offer up prayers to him, as well as to hear the preaching of the minister.

You often hear people say, "I liked that sermon," or, "I did not like that srmon this morning." Did you ever hear any one say, "I enjoyed that psalm or chapter that the minister read this morning, and the hymns and the prayers?" If you remember that in church you are in a place dedicated to God, for his worship—that we come here to pray, to sing praises and to hear what God has to say to us, rather than what a man may say, you will see that all ought to come to church every Sunday. All who are not detained at home by being sick or to take care of the sick, or by other necessary things, should be here to worship God and learn his will.

All ought to come to church, because God meets us here in a special way and blesses us as he blesses us nowhere else. It is here that God speaks to us in his blessed word and through his Spirit, and gives us evidence that he pardons our sins and will keep us from temptation. Here we learn what God wants us to do; and if we love God, we will seek to learn what he desires us to do to please him.

Be sure to come to God's house every Sunday when it is possible for you to be here. Come here remembering that it is God's house; that here we hear God's Book read; that here we pray with God's people; that

15. Going to Church

here we sing praises to God. Don't think of the minister and the sermons he preaches so much as you do of God and what HE says to us. In this way you will soon learn to love God's house. Instead of wanting to stay away, you will be glad to come to the place where God is worshiped.

16. The Bible

"From a child thou hast known the holy Scriptures, which are able to make thee wise unto salvation."—2 Tim. 3:14.

EVERY child loves stories. God knows that, and that's why God has made his book so full of stories. He intended it as the story-book for children always. This verse tells us about Timothy. He was a little Hebrew boy, and he learned the very Bible stories that you learn from your mothers. All the children of the Hebrews learned these stories. The result was that the best boys and girls in the whole world were to be found among the Hebrew children.

16. The Bible

Now I want to talk with you this morning a little about these holy Scriptures and your own reading of them.

You learn a good many stories that are in the Bible long before you can read them for yourselves, and you enjoy those stories, then, when someone else reads or tells them to you. But I have noticed that a great many boys and girls who can read for themselves hardly ever open a Bible except in the Sunday-school. A great many of you never have a Bible even there.

I. The first thing, then, I wish you to remember is, to *bring your Bible with you to church, prayer-meeting and Sabbath-school.* Leave your lesson-papers and quarterlies and question books at home. Carry your Bible with you. Let it be seen; don't be ashamed to be seen carrying a Bible. The fact that you have a Bible in your hand, or under your arm, has an influence on others for good. Mr. Moody tells of a man in London who went through a very wicked neighborhood every Sunday on his way to church, and he always carried his Bible under his arm. Mr. Moody said that Bible was a sermon half a mile long every Sunday.

But some of you may say, "I have no Bible of my own." Then buy one. If you have no money, ask your parents for one, and they will be glad to get for you a Bible that you can call your own.

II. The next thing is, *use your Bible*. There are a great many people who have plenty of Bibles but never use them. There are people, you know, who buy what they call a "family Bible," full of fine pictures, but it is a great mistake to call such Bibles family Bibles. The families never use them, and the children are hardly ever allowed even to look at the pictures—they think the book too fine, too nice to be looked at. Such Bibles are of no use: they are merely a piece of ornamental furniture. God intended us to use Bibles, not merely to put them on centre-tables for visitors to look at the beautiful binding.

1. Use your Bible *in the church* by turning to the place that is read, and following the minister as he reads; by turning to the text and marking it in the margin.

2. Use your Bible *in the Sabbath-school*. Don't bring anything but your Bible to the class. *The Bible*, not a Testament merely.

16. The Bible

And then *in the prayer meeting,* where we read together, you need your Bible.

3. Use your Bible most of all *in your home.* At family worship follow your father or mother in the reading, or let them allow you to read a verse in turn. Use your Bible by yourself *in your own room,* or anywhere. Take up your Bible and read it for yourself. Learn to love the places that interest you most. Read even though you may not understand. Read so that you may find things you can't understand, and may have questions to ask your father and mother, or Sunday-school teacher or pastor.

If you do this you will learn to love your Bible. You will reverence it and feel that it is God's letter to you; that it contains the word of life and is able to make you wise unto salvation.

THE END

Christian Classics *for* Young Readers

"I will keep you"

EMMA N. JANVIER, *Madeleine and the Lost Bracelet*
JOHN C. HILL, *The Children's Sermon*

THE REV. JOHN C. HILL served for several years as the pastor of the Presbyterian Church of Fayetteville, NY. According to *Frank Leslie's Sunday Magazine, Vol. XII (July–December 1882)*, he dissolved his pastoral relationship effective October 1, 1882, in order to serve as a missionary to China. There are reasons to doubt the accuracy of that report, however, since *The Presbyterian Monthly Record, Vol. 33*, records his missionary destination as Guatemala la Neuva, Guatemala. His appointment to Guatemala appears to be confirmed by the *Annual Report of the Presbyterian Church in the USA Board of Foreign Missions, Vol. 46*, p 115. His evangelical vision for Christian missions is recorded in *The Gospel in All Lands, Vol. VI (July–December 1882)*, pp. 83-84.

§

TIMOTHY MATTHEW SLEMMONS is *Professor of Homiletics and Worship* at the University of Dubuque Theological Seminary. In addition to several worship resources, homiletical writings, and his recent translation of the *Sermons on the First Epistle of John*, by the Swiss Reformer Johannes Oecolampadius, his books include *The Freedom of Christ: Sermons on Galatians*, and the illustrated stories, *The Secret of Salix Babylonicus: A Parable of the Weeping Willow* and *A Phenomenal Llama: A Tall Christmas Tale for Children of All Ages*, inspired by the intergenerational Christmas sermons of the late David H. C. Read.

Made in the USA
Coppell, TX
15 July 2020